Invasive Species

Jo Bourne

Illustrated by **Adam Howling**

OXFORD
UNIVERSITY PRESS

Contents

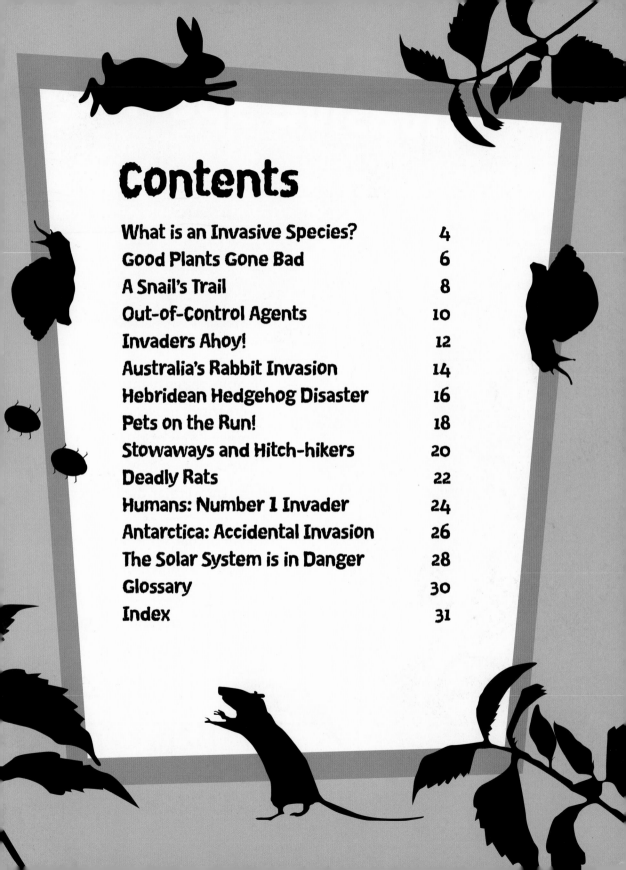

What is an Invasive Species?

There are millions of different life forms on Earth today. Each one has **evolved** to fit the place where it lives. This place is called a habitat.

Sometimes plants and creatures move, or get moved, out of their old habitat into a new one. Here, they either die or survive.

The problem is that some **species** like their new home so much they take over. As time passes, they can kill, eat or push out **native** plants and animals. They become an invasive species.

Invasive species do not mean to be pests – they are just trying to survive in their new homes. But as well as causing problems for the environment around them, they can damage buildings and even harm people.

New invasive species are settling into new neighbourhoods all the time. Nobody knows what incredible life forms might be discovered in the future, or where. But for now, come and investigate the invaders who could be creeping into *your* habitat!

Good Plants Gone Bad

Kudzu came from China and Japan and is called 'the vine that ate the south'. Since 1876, it has been spreading across the south-east of the United States of America (USA). Kudzu will grow over anything in its path.

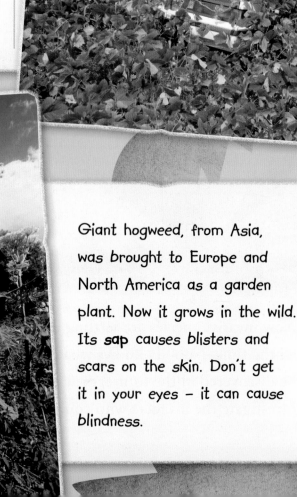

Giant hogweed, from Asia, was brought to Europe and North America as a garden plant. Now it grows in the wild. Its **sap** causes blisters and scars on the skin. Don't get it in your eyes – it can cause blindness.

Siam weed, or devil weed, is poisonous to animals. It has tiny hairy seeds that spread by sticking to animals and people. The plant first escaped from **botanical gardens** in India, and then invaded rainforests in Africa and damaged crops in the **tropics**.

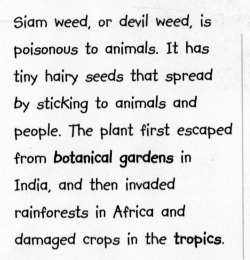

Water hyacinth from the Amazon basin has spread to **waterways** all over the world. It grows in a thick layer over lakes and rivers, and reduces their **oxygen** levels. This kills the creatures in the water.

A Snail's Trail

Giant African land snails come from East Africa. **Colonies** of these snails now live in China, Japan, India, the West Indies, Hawaii and other parts of the USA. These snails eat crops and even chew through plaster walls! What's worse, their waste can spread diseases to plants, animals and humans.

to Japan
11 000 kilometres

to Florida
13 000 kilometres

to China
8000 kilometres

to Hawaii
20 000 kilometres

to the West Indies
12 000 kilometres

to India
5000 kilometres

Look how far we've travelled!

If these snails can't move faster than 3 metres per hour, how have they spread so far?

A Snails and their eggs got inside ships travelling around the world.

B Snails were brought in as food.

C Snails were brought in as pets.

D Snails and their eggs floated down rivers on mats of tangled plants.

E Snails stuck to cars and lorries driving across **continents**.

The snails were spread in all these different ways.

FACT FILE

The largest Giant African land snail ever found had a shell that was 27.3 centimetres long!

Out-of-Control Agents

Biological Control Agents (BCAs) sound like top-secret government workers.
In fact, they can be anything from a beetle to a **fungus**, as long as they are the natural enemy of an invasive species.

The idea is to bring BCAs from their original location to the place where the invasive species has taken over. Then release the BCAs and let them kill the invaders. Sometimes it works, sometimes it doesn't ...

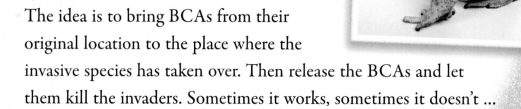

1 In the 1930s, farmers in Australia faced ruin when their sugar crops were attacked by the cane grub and beetle.

2 Scientists suggested importing cane toads from Hawaii to catch and eat the grubs.

3

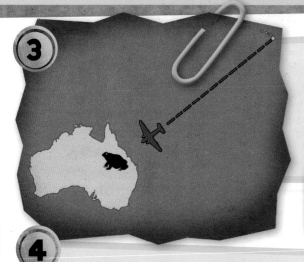

In 1935, 101 toads were flown in and left to breed. Later that year, 3000 young toads were released.

Cane toads hopped this far west by 2008.

4

The toads didn't eat the grubs. Instead they bred in their millions and became a major pest. Today, there may be as many as 200 million cane toads in Australia.

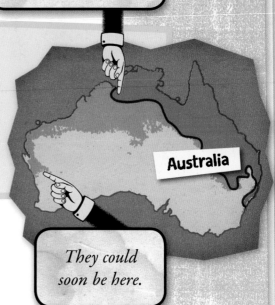

Australia

They could soon be here.

Oops!

5

And what about the cane grubs and beetles? They were killed by **pesticides** in the 1940s.

RIP
CANE GRUB
& BEETLE
1945

Invaders Ahoy!

Ships that carry goods around the world also carry ballast – heavy stuff that helps keep them **stable**. Ballast is often just seawater, kept in big tanks below deck.

Ships suck up seawater in one port, sail round the world and empty it in another port, thousands of miles away. But thousands of creatures get sucked up too ...

North America

South America

FACT FILE

Right now, ships all over the world are carrying the seeds, **spores**, **plankton**, **bacteria**, eggs and **larvae** of about 7000 different species.

I can eat ten times my own body weight in one day!

Spotted: North American comb jellyfish in the Black Sea – slow-moving with no brain, but **stealthy** hunters.

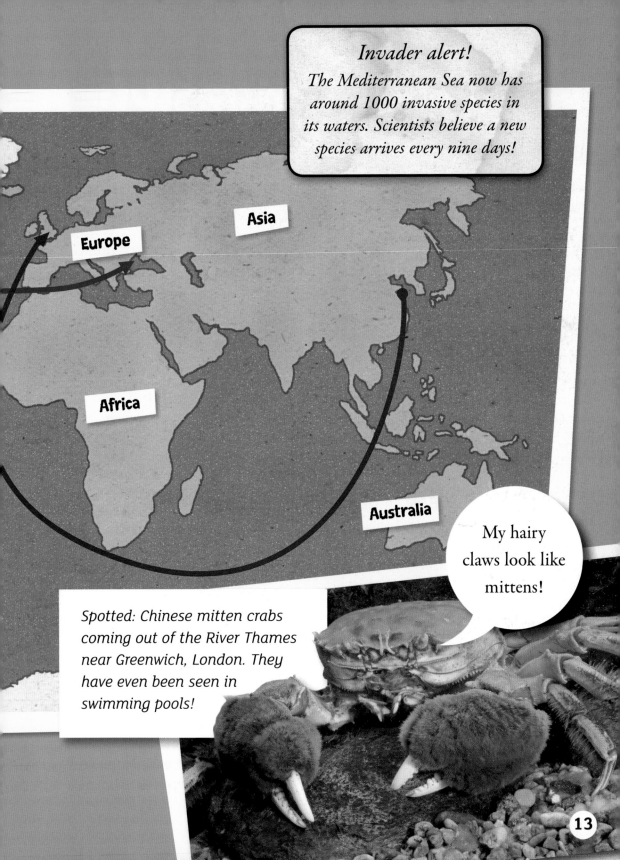

Invader alert!
The Mediterranean Sea now has around 1000 invasive species in its waters. Scientists believe a new species arrives every nine days!

Asia

Europe

Africa

Australia

My hairy claws look like mittens!

Spotted: Chinese mitten crabs coming out of the River Thames near Greenwich, London. They have even been seen in swimming pools!

13

Australia's Rabbit Invasion

English settler Thomas Austin releases 24 wild English rabbits in Victoria, Australia. The rabbits start breeding.

Rabbits reach Western Australia and Northern Territory.

Fences complete. Patrolled by bicycle riders, then camel riders, horse riders and cars.

More than two million rabbits are shot, but the population still grows.

To stop the spread of rabbits to Western Australia, work on the Number 1 Rabbit-Proof Fence begins.

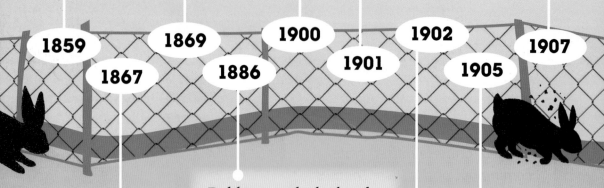

1859

1867

1869

1886

1900

1901

1902

1905

1907

Escaped rabbits eat plants and become a pest.

Rabbits reach the border between Queensland and New South Wales.

Work starts on the Number 2 Fence. Later, work starts on the Number 3 Fence.

Rabbits are found west of fence line.

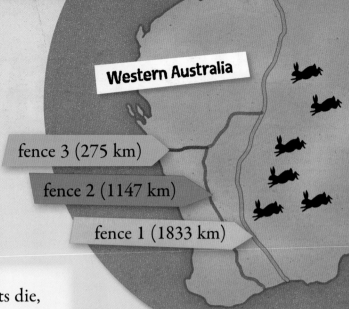

Western Australia

fence 3 (275 km)

fence 2 (1147 km)

fence 1 (1833 km)

Rabbits cover
four million
square kilometres
of Australia.

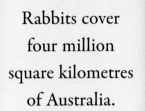

Millions of rabbits die,
but the survivors are more
resistant to disease.

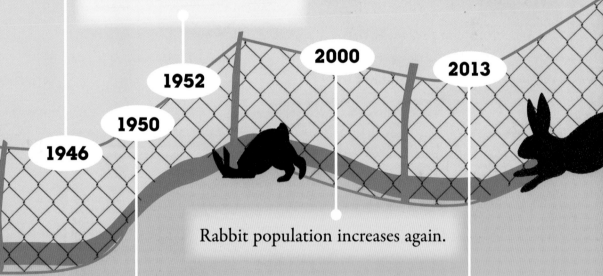

2000

1952

1950

1946

2013

Rabbit population increases again.

Rabbit population is
600 million. Scientists release
the deadly disease **myxomatosis**
to kill the rabbits.

Rabbits are still a pest.
The government plans
to extend the fence.

Hebridean Hedgehog Disaster

In 1974, a few hedgehogs were brought from mainland Britain into a garden on the Hebrides, off the west coast of Scotland. The gardener hoped they would eat slugs and snails.

The Hebrides

mainland Britain

There were no badgers (which eat hedgehogs), pesticides, or busy roads to cross on the island. The hedgehog population soon grew to 5000.

The hedgehogs spread over the Hebrides islands. They ate small creatures, and when the **wading bird** population decreased, hedgehogs were blamed for eating their eggs.

FLY HOME THE HEDGEHOGS SAVE THE WADERS

A hedgehog **cull** began to reduce their numbers but thousands of hedgehogs survived. On mainland Britain, the hedgehog was becoming an endangered species. So it was decided to trap the hedgehogs on the Hebrides and move them to the mainland. Over the years, around 1600 hedgehogs have been transported by ferry.

Exotic animals have been kept as pets since the Middle Ages, but sometimes they get away from their owners! Here are four of the most invasive – look out for them!

Muntjac deer

Original home:	South-east China
Escaped from:	Deer parks and zoos
New home:	Republic of Ireland and the UK
Threat:	They can cause car accidents and destroy woodland.

Ring-necked parakeet

Original home:	India, Asia and Africa
Escaped from:	People's homes
New home:	London/south-east England
Threat:	They are noisy and can damage crops.

Sacred ibis

Original home:	Southern Africa
Escaped from:	Zoos and parks
New home:	France, Italy and Florida (USA)
Threat:	They feed on the eggs of crocodiles and birds.

Burmese python

Original home:	Southern Asia
Escaped from:	People's homes
New home:	Florida (USA)
Threat:	They eat wildlife, including alligators!

Stowaways and Hitch-hikers

WANTED

HAVE YOU SEEN THESE PESTS?

Asian long-horned beetle

From: Asia
Pest in: USA, Europe and Canada
Arrival: In wood packing cases aboard ships.
Damage caused: Kills trees by burrowing into them.

Indian house crow

From: India
Pest in: The Netherlands and Florida (USA)
Arrival: Hitches a ride on passing ships.
Damage caused: Destroys crops and native birds.

Spanish slug

From: South-west Europe
Pest in: Europe
Arrival: Hitch-hikes on plants and in plant pots.
Damage caused: Eats crops; carries **parasites**.

Colorado beetle

From: Mexico
Pest in: USA, Europe and parts of Asia
Arrival: With fresh vegetables from other countries.
Damage caused: Eats crops – potatoes, tomatoes and peppers.

Western flower thrip

From: North America
Pest in: Whole world except Antarctica
Arrival: With garden plants from other countries.
Damage caused: Destroys flowers and vegetables in greenhouses.

Deadly Rats

This is a black rat. It is small with a hairless tail longer than its body. Rats spread all over Europe, but they don't travel alone ...

Black rats come from South-east Asia and India. They eat almost anything and breed quickly. They like living close to humans because they can always find food nearby.

Black rats began travelling through Europe in Roman times. When people started trading by ship, the rats hopped on board and spread even faster.

Rats carry diseases in their blood.
They also carry fleas. When rats
die, the fleas – still filled with rats'
blood – hop off and bite people.
Then people get the rats' diseases.

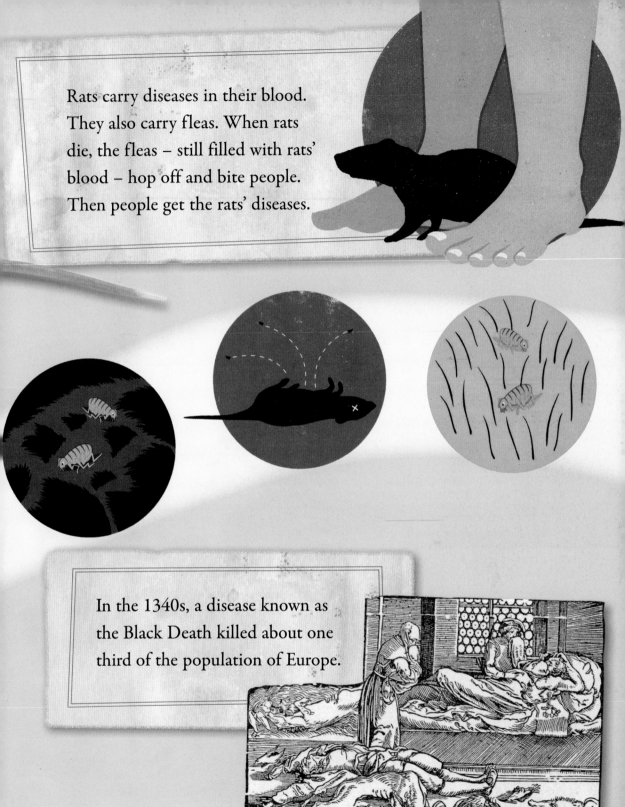

In the 1340s, a disease known as
the Black Death killed about one
third of the population of Europe.

Humans: Number 1 Invader

Of all the world's invasive species, there is one true champion. It's us – humans!

Our ancestors in Africa evolved around 200 000 years ago. Around 60 000 years ago they started travelling and never stopped. They built boats to cross seas.

12 000 years ago, humans started farming. Animals and plants were exchanged around the world.

Now humans live in every hot, cold, wet and dry place on Earth. Our numbers are increasing all the time.

How humanity has grown

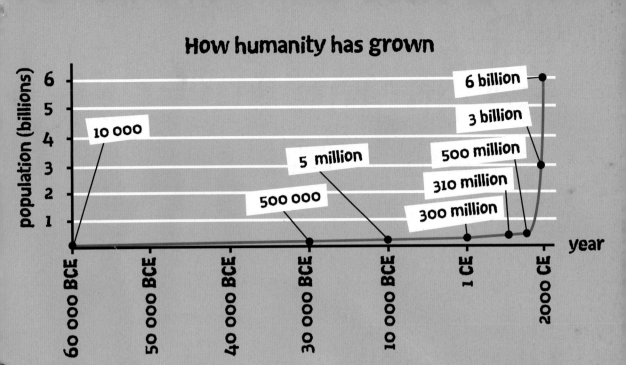

population (billions)

- 6 billion
- 3 billion
- 500 million
- 310 million
- 300 million
- 5 million
- 500 000
- 10 000

year

60 000 BCE   50 000 BCE   40 000 BCE   30 000 BCE   10 000 BCE   1 CE   2000 CE

Humans take what they need from the planet. Like all the species in this book, they do everything they can to survive.

Right now, humans are the world's greatest success story, but everywhere we go we make a terrible mess. We need to be very clever and inventive in the future to clear up our mess.

Don't forget that humans carry insects and **viruses** wherever they go!

25

Antarctica: Accidental Invasion

Antarctica is a vast and icy island continent. It is cut off from the rest of the world by hundreds of kilometres of ocean. It is the last pure environment on the planet.

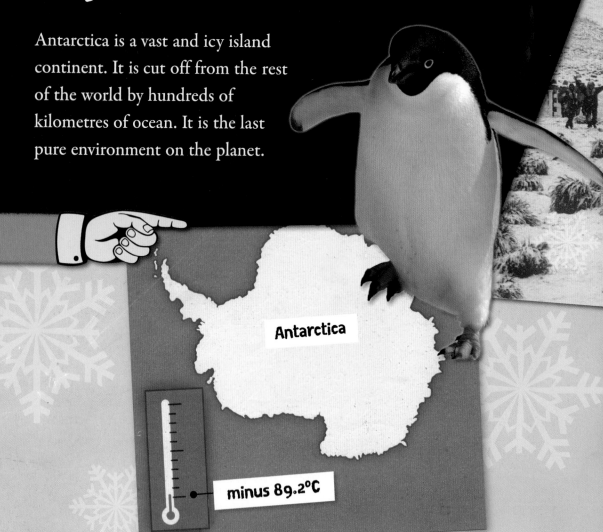

Antarctica

minus 89.2°C

Temperatures here can fall to far below freezing – down to minus 89.2°C! That makes Antarctica the coldest place on Earth. Not many creatures live on the land and there are hardly any plants. But this is changing ...

Each year, up to 5000 scientists and around 40 000 tourists visit Antarctica. They accidentally bring mud on their boots and seeds on their clothes. Spiders, beetles, ants, moths and more have all been found at science research stations.

So far, the worst invader is a tiny midge (a small fly). It makes burrows in the soil. These burrows make it easier for plants to grow. Scientists don't know what will happen next – plants might start growing everywhere!

Africa

South America

Antarctica

Australia

New Zealand

The Solar System is in Danger

From us! There is a real danger to the solar system from Earth. **Microscopic** life forms called bacteria can survive for over a year in space. We don't want to find life on Mars, then discover it was carried from Earth because it was stuck to a spacecraft. We also don't want to change a planet by introducing Earth life to it.

What's the answer?

NASA bakes its spacecraft before take-off! They use ovens that 'cook' the spacecraft at 112°C for 30 hours. The heat kills microscopic life!

Quarantine!

When the first men to walk on the Moon arrived home in 1969, they were put into quarantine for 21 days. This means they were kept apart from other humans and animals. Their landing module and samples were also put into quarantine. No **microbes** from space were ever found.

So while the plants and animals on our planet are busy getting all mixed up, space is safe – for now!

Glossary

bacteria: tiny living things that can cause disease

botanical gardens: gardens where plants from all over the world are grown for scientific study and education

colonies: groups of animals or plants that live or grow together

continents: the Earth's big land areas

cull: the organized killing of a particular kind of animal

evolved: changed and developed over time

fungus: a plant which breaks down dead matter

larvae: young insects that will have a different form as adults

microbes: tiny living things which can only be seen with a microscope and can cause disease

microscopic: very tiny, invisible to the naked eye

myxomatosis: an infectious disease that affects rabbits and usually kills them

NASA: the American agency in charge of space exploration

native: belonging to a certain area

oxygen: the part of the air that living things need to breathe

parasites: creatures which live on or inside other creatures

pesticides: chemicals that kill plant or animal pests

plankton: tiny sea animals that are eaten by larger sea animals

sap: the liquid that moves around inside a plant

species: groups of animals or plants that are similar

spores: cells that can reproduce by themselves

stable: balanced and unlikely to topple over

stealthy: doing something secretly and quietly

tropics: the region of the Earth around the equator

viruses: tiny living things, smaller than bacteria, that can cause disease

wading bird: a bird which walks in shallow water to look for food

waterways: lakes, rivers or canals that boats can travel on